NLP

AND

MANIPULATION:

The simple guide to use NLP techniques

and manipulation

Oliver Bennet

Table of Contents

Chapter 1:   Deception 1

Chapter 2:   Hypnosis.. 7

Chapter 3:   Reverse Psychology 13

Chapter 4:   Seduction.. 17

Chapter 5:   The NLP Negotiator: Effective Tactics 24

Chapter 6:   The Impact of Being in a Manipulative
Relationship 31

Chapter 7:   Media Manipulation: Strategies and How to See
Through Them.. 38

Chapter 8:   Why Self-Discipline And Self-Control Are
Important?   42

Chapter 9:   The Sustainability Of An Excellent Emotional
State Of Mind 50

Chapter 10:   Embracing Our Feelings... 57

Chapter 11:   Reflect On The Bright Side Of Life Everyday .. 63

Chapter 12:   Ways To Attract Good Energy 69

Chapter 13:   Daily Emotional Management Rituals.............. 74

Conclusion 80

Chapter 1:   Deception

Deception is another key aspect that comes with dark psychology. Like many other tactics that come with dark psychology, it is sometimes difficult to tell whether one instance of deception is considered dark or not. But before we explore more into this, we need first to understand what deception is all about in our world.

Deception will be any word or action capable of making someone believe something that is not true. Fraudulently providing evidence for something false, implying falsehood, omitting the truth, and lying are all examples of deception.

Not all types of deception will count as dark psychology. Everyone will deceive others to some extent or another they may deceive others. They feel inadequate, because they feel embarrassed, or even as a kindness. For example, some studies have shown that many men are going to lie about their heights. This doesn't mean that they practice dark psychology. Besides, it is common for people to deceive themselves about various issues such as happiness, ambition, and health.

The Deception Spectrum

Deception can happen either on a small or large scale. Many people assume that deception has to occur on a large scale to be important. But dark deception is present in all parts of the spectrum, and it is important to be on the lookout at all times to ensure that you are safe.

Dark deceivers will often use the smaller deceptions to help them out as well. They may start with some of these small deceptions to test out the victim and condition that victim to believe the larger lies the deceiver uses later on.

Smaller deceptions can also be carried out to undermine the victim's trust in their powers of reason and logic. Suppose the manipulator can deceive the victim over a smaller issue, and the victim starts to question what is happening. In that case, the victim may conclude that their suspicion is irrational, and they cannot trust their judgment. Most people will start to conclude that it is their judgment that is at fault here, rather than entertaining the idea that someone else is deceiving them over some issue that seems so small. Of course, the dark deceiver is aware of this trust that people generally have and will try to exploit it.

A dark deceiver can work with a large-scale deception as well. One of the largest deceptions that they can use is to convince someone that you are someone else. Not in terms of just a personality trait or some other small detail. A true deceiver can even hide their entire identity. They will hide their date of birth, their name, and everything else. This is done to help push forward the goals or the agenda of the manipulator.

Deceptive Topics

Everyone has heard the saying "Money is the root of all evil." This may seem like an exaggeration, but money can often be the root of various deceptions. Deception and money more often than not cross paths. Some people will deceive in the hopes of attaining money; others will do it to hide their money, and so much more. Because money shows up as a topic so often when it comes to deception, we will take a look at it now.

Take a look at a professional beggar. These individuals will try to get money from the public, even though they have plenty of their own. These beggars will use a few different dark psychological principles to get the money they want from their innocent victims.

2

Such beggars are even willing to put some injuries on their bodies to look more desperate.

Personal marital status is another area where people are going to deceive. Sometimes, a person may try to hide their married background to seducing a new victim. This could be for sexual or financial reasons. Even other people have multiple wives that are spread out across the world, wives who have no idea about each other. This deception type has become even harder with the beginning of the Internet and can check in on people through social media. These deceivers can manage more than one wife from each other through many different means.

Some people may appear to be falsely married when they are not. A married couple is often seen as more trustworthy than one who is not married. The dark manipulator is aware of this idea and may choose to use it for their own end goals. Some people may try to have a pretend marriage to help with taxes and insurance. One of the most common deception types with this is when the deceiver creates a fictional dead wife or husband to sympathize with those around them and often their money.

A deceiver may also try to hide their criminal background. This is because it is hard to be trusted, either personally or professionally, to commit certain crimes. Many manipulators feel like they can use deception to hide any socially unacceptable or abnormal feelings. This can stop the victim from being alerted to the person they are dealing with until it is way too late.

For example, a dark manipulator may decide that they only want to use their victim for sex. But they know that if they focus on this topic, it will be a red flag and hard for them to get what they want. They then decide to deceive the victim. They may overtly lie and then imply that their true intention here is commitment and love.

The victim will fall for this deception, the exploitation from that manipulator is done, and then the victim is the one harmed by the deception.

In a romantic relationship, the manipulator is often going to hide their true intentions. Deceptive actions and words will leave the victim feeling that the other person is exactly what they were looking for at that moment in time. This happens because the manipulator can identify someone who is vulnerable and then probe into their needs and weak points. The manipulator can then use this information and then cloak themselves so they appear to be something they aren't. This is a common beginning with the manipulator that can turn into more long-term manipulations that the victim isn't aware of.

Deceptive Tactics

The first deceptive tactic that can be used is lying. This is the first technique that the manipulator will choose as soon as they know that the victim is susceptible to lies and has trouble figuring out the truth. This is often because the victim is someone who trusts others. Or the manipulator may have worked on this victim for some time so that they lower their guard. The manipulator can also find ways to hide up the lies and then explain the discrepancies if the victim starts to notice.

Any deception that occurs with lying is likely to occur in a very subtle way and is thought out ahead of time. A deceiver is going to embed their lie into some truthful information. For example, the manipulator would start with a story that is about ninety percent true and ten percent false. Because it sounds legitimate and most of the story can be proven as true, the victim will think it is true.

Implying is another form of deception. Implying is when the manipulator is going to suggest something false is true rather than boldly stating it. If the manipulator wants to deceive a victim about how much money they have, they could either lie or imply it. A lie would be something like "Oh I'm a successful guy. I've made a lot of money," even though the manipulator knows this information is not true. But when they imply they are rich, they may say something like "it's so stressful trying to handle things with my accountant. Trying to get my tax bill down takes a lot of my time." The manipulator has acted and spoken in a way that makes the other person think they are wealthy, but they never state it.

Omission is another option for the deceiver. This is a failure to mention something, usually a fact that is pretty important, that is true. Omission doesn't use a falsehood to cover the truth like the other two options. Instead, this one is going to ignore the truth or just leave it out. Often this piece of information is important for the victim to know about to make an informed decision. The manipulator would leave this out to protect themselves and ensure that the victim didn't have all the information.

One way that the deceiver can use omission is to create their own emotional fence with that situation. This is a tactic where the manipulator implies that a particular period of their life, or some particular topic, is painful or uncomfortable for them to discuss. The victim, feeling bad and wanting to be considerate, will avoid bringing up this topic. This gives the manipulator a chance to avoid the truth while still making the victim feel guilty when trying to bring up that painful topic.

And the final form of deception will be the most elaborate, and often criminal, form. This is known as fraud. Instead of the deceiver simply lying about something from the past, this kind of deceit will have false stories, documents, and some other evidence to back up whatever their lie says. The deceiver is going to use these things subtly. They would never say something like "I'm a doctor; take a look at my certificate!"

Instead, they will use some subtle displays to show off to the victim. They will try to steer away from being too pushy with their fraudulent claims because they know that doing this will make the victim feel that something is wrong with the situation.

Fraud is becoming more common than ever because of the Internet. Deceivers can often work with professional software to make documents that look pretty realistic, no matter what type of document they need. This can make it hard to tell whether you are working with someone telling you the truth or deceiving you.

When this dark deception starts to enter the realm of fraudulence, it can be a bad sign. It shows that the deceiver is dangerous and they are committed to sticking with that dark psychology. They are risking serious criminal charges to do this kind of manipulation, and they are confident that they can do this without anyone noticing it at all.

Chapter 2:   Hypnosis

What Is Hypnosis?

There have been many definitions of what hypnosis is. The American Psychological Association has defined hypnosis as a cooperative collaboration where the hypnotist will give suggestions to the person; he picks which he or she will respond to. Edmonton said that a person is but in a deep state of mind when in undergoing hypnosis. Therefore, hypnosis is when a person enters a state of mind in which a person finds himself or herself vulnerable to the suggestions of a hypnotist. Hypnosis is not new to us because many people have seen it in movies, cartoons or been to magic shows or performances where participants are told to do usual acts and they do it. One thing is for sure that, some people do believe that hypnosis exist and would do anything to avoid being a victim while others believe that its fiction.

Induction

Induction is considered as stage one of hypnosis. There are three stages in total. Induction aims to intensify the partaker's expectations of what follows after, explaining the role they will be playing, seeking their attention and any other steps needed during this stage. There are many methods used by hypnotists to induce a participant to hypnosis. One of them is the "Braidism" technique which requires a hypnotist to follow a few steps. This technique is named after James Braid. First step would be to find a bright object and hold it in your left hand and specifically between the middle, fore, and thumb fingers. The object should be placed where the participant will be able to fix their stare and maintain the stare. This position would be the above the forehead. It is always important that the hypnotist remind the partaker to keep their eyes on the object. If the participant wonders away from the object, the process will not work. The participant should be completely focused on the object. The participant's eyes will begin to dilate and the participant will begin to have a wavy motion. A hypnotist will know that his participant is in a trance when the participant involuntarily closes his or her eyelids when the middle and fore fingers of the right hand are carried from the eyes to the object. When this does not happen, the participant is begins again being guided that their eyes are to close when the fingers are used in a similar motion. Therefore, this puts the participant in an altered state of mind he or she is said to be hypnotized. The induction technique has been considered not to be necessary for every case and research has shown that this stage is not as important as previously had been known when it came to the effects of induction technique. Over the years, there have been variations in the once original hypnotic induction technique while others have preferred to use other alternatives. James Braid innovation of this technique still stands out.

Suggestion

After Induction, the next stage that follows is the suggestion stage. James Braid left out the word suggestion when he first defined hypnosis. He, however, described this stage as attempting to draw the partaker's conscious mind to focus on one central idea. James Braid would start by minimizing the functions of different parts of the partaker's body. He would then put more emphasis on the use of verbal and non-verbal suggestions to begin to get the partaker into a hypnotic state. Hippolyte Bernheim also shifted from the physical state of the partaker. This well-known hypnotist described hypnosis as the induction of a peculiar physical condition that increases one's susceptibility to the participant's suggestions. Suggestions can be verbal or one that doesn't involve speech. Modern hypnotist uses different form of suggestions that include non-verbal cues, direct verbal suggestions, metaphors and insinuations. Non-verbal suggestions that may be used include changing the tone, mental imagery and physical manipulation. Mental imagery can take two forms. One includes those that are delivered with permission and those that are done none the less and are more authoritarian.

When discussing hypnosis, it would be wise if one would be able to distinguish between the conscious mind and unconscious mind. Most hypnosis while using suggestions will trigger the conscious mind other than the unconscious mind. In contrast, other hypnotists will view it as way of communicating with the unconscious mind. Hypnotists such as Hippolyte Bernheim and James Braid and other great hypnotists see it as trying to communicate with the conscious mind. This is what they believed. James Braid even defines hypnosis as the attention that is focused upon the suggestion. The idea that a hypnotist will be able to invade into your unconscious mind and order you around is next to impossible as according to those who belong to Braids school of thought. The determinant of the different conceptions about suggestions has also been the nature of the mind.

Hypnotists such as Milton Erickson believe that responses given are normally through the unconscious mind and they used the case of indirect suggestions as an example. Many of the nonverbal suggestions such as metaphors will mask the hypnotist's true intentions from the conscious mind of the victim. A form of hypnosis that is completely reliant upon the unconscious theory is subliminal suggestion. Where the unconscious mind is left out in the hypnosis process then this form of hypnosis would be impossible. The distinction between the two schools of thoughts is quite easy to decipher. The first school of thought believe that suggestions are directed at the conscious mind will use verbal suggestions.

In contrast, the second school of thought who believe that suggestions are directed at the unconscious mind will use metaphors and stories that mask their true intentions. In general, the participant will still need to draw their attentions to an object or idea. This enables the hypnotist to lead the participant in the direction that the hypnotist will need to go into the hypnotic state. Once this stage of suggestion is completed and is successful, the participant will move onto the next stage.

Susceptibility

It has been shown that people are more likely to fall prey of the hypnotist tactics than others will. Therefore, it will be noted that some people can fall into hypnosis easily and the hypnotist does not have to put so much effort. At the same time, for some, getting into the hypnotic stage may take longer and require the hypnotist to put quite the effort. While for some even after the hypnotist's continued efforts, they will not get into the hypnotic state. Research has shown where a person has been able to reach the hypnotic state at some point in their lives then it is likely that they will be susceptible to the hypnotist's suggestions and those who have not been hypnotized or it has always been difficult for them to reach that state then it will be likely that they may never be able to reach that hypnotic state.

Different models have been established to determine susceptibility of partakers to hypnosis. Research done by Deirdre Barrett showed that there are two types of subjects that considered being more susceptible to hypnosis and its effects. The two subjects consist of the group of dissociates and fantasizers.

10

Fantasizers can easily block out the stimuli from reality without the specific use of hypnosis. They day dream a lot and also spent their childhood believing in the existence of imaginary friends. Dissociates are persons who have scarred childhoods. They have experienced trauma or child abuse and found ways to put away the past and become numb. If a person belongs to this group finds him or herself day dreaming, then it will be associated with being blank and creating fantasies. These two groups will have the highest rates of being hypnotized.

Types of Hypnosis

A hypnotist can use different types of hypnosis a participant. Each of them will use different ways and will help with certain issues. Some types of hypnosis will assist in weight loss while others will be used to help a participant relax.

Traditional Hypnosis

This type of hypnosis is very popular and used by hypnotists. It works by the hypnotist making suggestions to the participant's unconscious mind. The participant that is likely to be hypnotized by this is one who does what he is told and does not ask many or frequent questions. If one was to self-hypnotize themselves, they will do this by using traditional hypnosis. Like we have said, this type of hypnosis is very popular and this could be attributed to it not requiring much skill and not technical. The hypnotist will just have the right words and just tell the participant what to do. This might pose a problem to the hypnotist where the participant is a critical thinker and can analyze a given situation.

Neuro-Linguistic Programming (NLP)

This type of hypnosis gives the hypnotist wide criteria for the methods they can use in hypnosis. The hypnotist can save time during the process as the hypnotist will just use the same thought patterns as the one that is creating the problem in the participant. If it is stress for example, the same thought pattern causing this stress will counter the stress.

Chapter 3:   Reverse Psychology

This is a strategy used by people to get what they want by asking or demanding what they do not want. Scientists use another term: self-anticonformity because your demand goes against what you want.

Another way that psychologists explain reverse psychology is through the term reactance. It refers to the uncomfortable feeling that people get when they feel that their freedom has been threatened. The normal way to respond to that threat is the opposite of what has been demanded of you. It's the going against authority aspect.

Examples of Reverse Psychology

Reverse psychology is prevalent in many different types of professions because it can help people get what they want. It can be productive and successful if executed right. For instance, some sales techniques are based on this very principle, such as the Door in the Face technique. We have all fallen victim to this. Let's say that you are in a used car lot trying to buy a car. The salesman gives you this outlandish price that you would never consider paying. You want to buy the car, but you do not want to pay that much. So, you make a counteroffer for less. This is exactly what the salesman wants. You get the smaller price and the salesman makes the sale, which was his goal in the first place - putting you in a car.

The tactic can also be used in marketing. Here is an example of a store that sells high-quality merchandise. When we go shopping, we see advertisements and the name of the store on the outside of the store. We know where we are going. Well, what if the high-end store has no signs or ads on the outside of the store. It just looks like a regular building. You would have to know where the store was or have been there before to know that they did sell clothes. We all know that this indicates that the retailer is not trying to sell to just anyone. This enhances the mystery of the place and it makes it an exclusive venue. Those who do not want to be excluded or comfortable with the exclusivity will want to buy from the store.

This is a tactic that can be used for good as well. For instance, a parent might use it to get their kid to eat their broccoli. We all know the story; the parent tells the kid to eat their vegetables because they are good. But the kid doesn't like them and won't eat them. It is like a constant battle. So, what does the parent do? They use this tactic by getting the kid to want to eat them. How do you they do that? Haven't you ever bought some sweets that you didn't want the kids to eat. You put them in the fridge and tell the kids that those belong to you and not touch them? What happens? The kid finds a way to eat sweets because they can't have them. They're yours. Why not try that tactic with the broccoli? See how fast the kid jumps on those because they can't have them. We always want what we can't have.

Using this tactic in relationships can be a bad thing if the person using the tactic is trying to get something at their partner's expense. For instance, you asked your partner to go to the store. But instead of asking them directly, you tell them that they cannot handle the traffic right now. They might go just to prove you wrong. If this becomes a normal occurrence, your partner might stop trusting what you're saying to them, become angry with you and start to believe that you are trying to manipulate them to get what you want. This could backfire because they might believe what you say and start becoming dependent on you.

So, does reverse psychology work? That depends on the people involved. First, the victim has to believe that the culprit wants them to do something before they react to their demands and do quite the opposite. If they are aware that you are using this tactic on them, then it is never going to work.

Who Can Fall Victim To Reverse Psychology?

Anyone can fall for any of these tactics because no one is safe from those who will do whatever it takes to get what they want from others. With this being said, those more relaxed and laid-back personalities don't usually fall for reverse psychology techniques.

So, who does fall more easily for reverse psychology tactics?

Those more irritable, stubborn, and overly emotional personalities will find that they fall for these tactics easier than others. Children are more susceptible as well because the cognitive parts of their brains have not fully developed yet. They might not perceive social cues that others can because they are less aware of what is going on. As they get older into their teen years, they might be able to sense what is going on, but they are also at the time in their lives trying to be more independent. However, they still have a strong urge to fight against authority and might do the opposite of what is asked of them just despite that.

How to Use Reverse Psychology

It might sound simple, demand the opposite of what you want. However, here are some steps for you, just in case.

1. Your victim needs to have at least heard of both options.
2. Argue against the option that you want

3.   Use nonverbal communication to back up what you are saying because it will make your case stronger.

Reverse psychology can be dangerous – especially if the victim finds out what you are doing, and if its motives are wrong. With that being said, it can be used for good – as shown above in the parent example. If you decide that you are going to use it, you should be careful and now what you are doing first and know the consequences of using the strategy. Sometimes a more clear, concise and direct approach could be better.

Chapter 4:   Seduction

This talks about a psychological process that deals with how people get into an intimate relationship or lead people astray to persuade by corrupting or inducing a person to engage in a sexual relationship. Like it is in any other aspect of dark psychology, people seduce others in other to get them to do what they want so that they can obtain their selfish goals.

The strategies used in seduction include sexual scripts, conversation, paralinguistic gestures and non-verbal means of communication, and other short-term behavioral strategies. The word seduction originates from a Latin word which means "leading astray." This means that the word "seduction" can have either a positive or a negative meaning.

Attraction

To attract powerfully is a strong definition of seduction. This is a skill like any other. It can be honed and worked on with experience and practice. The things that attract us are indeed unique, however, some basic things attract us all. Like comfort and stability. Most find these things to be very attractive. Those who can provide it, or the illusion of it, can indeed persuade us. This is a form of allure. Allure is the quality of attraction. It is the thing that draws us. Allure is a powerful accomplice to seduction. They go hand in hand. Seduction being the act, and the allure being the draw.

In speaking of the act there is a lure when it comes to seduction. A lure is something that baits something. It is the morsel at the end of the string. When used properly, the lure can pull individuals from where they are to where the person on the other end of seduction wants them to be. And there are many forms of the lure. One being...

Temptation

To tempt is the attraction to the things that are not necessarily beneficial to us. This can be an indicator of darkness, although not necessarily. When we are tempted by something, we need to stop and look at what is tempting us and why. The temptation is the reasoning behind the attraction. It is often logical and explains the lure in an innocent light.

A more mellow version of the temptation is the entice. The entice is the offering of pleasure or advantage. It is more formal than the temptation, yet it is less pressuring. Enticement shows its hand by showing you what is possible. Enticement does not necessarily lead to seduction.

Beguile

When we talk about the enchantment of beguile, we begin to stumble into deception. This is a form of seduction for sure. It is not simply the seducing part of the process. Beguile is included with trickery to get what is needed. This can be considered very dark, and the ability to deceive is practiced by those who manipulate.

The saying is that flattery will get you everywhere and anything. This is the urge we talked about in manipulation and persuasion. This flattery is praise of the intent. Truth comes into play when it comes to being influenced. False flattery can show dark intentions. When we are being flattered, we are being moved by this flattery. Wheel, and flatter, it is the movement of seduction.

When we are unable to move, we are considered to be trapped. Ensnarement can happen during seduction in everything from actual handcuffs to the ensnarement of the heart and mind. It is the freeze of the hunted—ensnared by seduction. The cornerstone of seduction is charm. Charm is the charismatic ability to bring about almost everything listed above. From flattery to allure, charm can be the core of it all. We have talked a little about charm when it comes to manipulation. Charm combined with seduction is deadly. Seduction captivates. It is the essence that draws us so that we cannot look away. When considering everything from the gruesome to the sublime, captivation is encompassing seduction. When we are captivated, we are not necessarily ensnared. One captivated is not as secure as one ensnared. The captivated can most likely walk away. Then seduction pulls out another card and enchants. The spell. There is no science here, there is only magic. This magic of enchantment is yet another form of seduction. Yes, enchantment is a lure, and an enticement for desire. It has another form. It's a wonderment that there is something bigger than what we already know. When we are enchanted, we get lost in what we know and do not know.

Hypnotize and mesmerize are part of seduction when removed from the practice of the art. This means that these concepts are not just the practiced art of putting someone into an altered state for the process of suggestion.

Think about it for a minute. Yes, they are. They are part of seduction.

Yet another reason to have difficulty in measuring the science of hypnotherapy. This gray area... it is prime for dark psychology.

Back to seduction. Seduction is about the tantalize. It is the torment or tease. The offering of the unobtainable. Achieving this unobtainable thing is not the goal of the tantalize. It is the process of seduction that defines it. Entice is the promise during seduction.

Seduction titillates. Titillation is the excitement we feel when we are being seduced. This tingling can be a little tickle to a grand encompassing distraction. There is an effect seduction has upon us. The physical sensation mixed with the mental makes seduction the wondering and destructive force that it is. If we do not watch out, we can become bewitched. Alongside enchantment and delight there is bewitched. We are once again going beyond the normal into the magical. Believe in magic or not, being bewitched takes on a role beyond titillation or even basic seduction. There is the magic of control here. A surrender to a force that is not definable. Being bewitched takes us out of ourselves and puts us into a place of controlled magic.

Or it could just be another word for enchantment.

When we turn up the volume of seduction, we start to get into ravaging. When we ravage another, it is almost a devouring. This is starting to become an even more destructive force. Ravage is part of seduction. Some like to be ravaged, and in this there is a surrender that can be relatively harmful. When we are trapped or lead astray, this is a prime opportunity to become trapped. The trap is most certifiably a part of seduction. From the innocent capture of someone's affections to the forcible complete surrender of a trapped animal, the trap is the conclusion of seduction.

It is extremely interesting how often we go to seduction. There is a belief that it is a combination of things. From the basic core drive of us to be part of a society, to the desire to be wanted, seduction takes us there. It also allows us to surrender to it. There is a peace in the surrender to another. A high of being trapped.

When an animal gets caged or trapped—no matter how evolved we get, humans are animals—when trapped or tied up we eventually get to a point where we know we cannot escape and vacate from ourselves. It is in this surrender that we feel the swept motion. Seduction can take us there, the trap leading to the sweep, and for some that is all life needs. For those who practice in the dark, this area is a primal hunting ground. To take down prey with seduction fulfills a very primal understanding of what emotion is. When both parties participate and understand ground rules, seduction is a playful thing. With darkness and the psychological ability to control and manipulate, our moments of emotions during seduction become very vulnerable.

Control

What happens after this seduction takes place? Is there a moment where seduction is not enough to keep controlling the prey? Yes, seduction only takes us so far in control. It can be re-administered with a balance of charm to ensnare prey again and again. Yet there are greater tools that the dark use to keep control over others when seduction begins to wear off.

One of these tools is the lie. Lies are complex, convoluted and honestly not defined due to the unlimited ways they can be used.

Lies are a control mechanism of dark psychology.

So, we had better take a look.

Seduction Techniques

Below are three common techniques that are used in the art of seduction:

Switch between being arrogant and humorous:

This will work for a man that is trying to seduce a woman. Once you have successfully gotten her to talk to you, you can then decide to be both cocky and funny. This should be a very simple thing to do. Be a tease but while at it, spice it up with a bit of arrogance. Look for those things that you can use to mock or taunt her but keep in mind that this must be light-hearted as you do not want to come off as though you are castigating her.

This could also work for a woman to a man, but men typically use it more on women. Regardless of the gender of the user, it is important to apply caution, as the careless use of this method can produce ripple effects. The whole idea is to come off as a funny person, so you do not want to end up hurting the other person in any way.

Try to know more about the other person by asking for some personal details:

It is important to remember that you do not want to ask questions that will bore the other person, so you must ask him or her about them. Make sure you don't end up digging a pit for yourself by asking questions that will never contribute in any way to arousing their interest in you.

The truth is that the kind of questions you ask are always a reflection of who you are, so be mindful of the questions you ask. Your questions should make the person laugh, they shouldn't be boring, and they should make the person want to talk more. So, even after the conversation has ended, they will continue to think about you.

Make use of some subtly sexy words/language:

When you are trying to seduce someone, the best way to hook them is by adding some spice to their interaction with you. To do this, you must use some subtle forms to broach certain sexual topics. It is flat out wrong to start talking about sexuality, like how people should engage in sex. You are expected to make use of subtle suggestions that will put the person at ease with you so that they are not insecure or uncomfortable when they are in your company. You do not want to have them avoiding you because of something you have said.

Chapter 5:   The   NLP   Negotiator: Effective Tactics

Life is full of negotiation, and you will have to negotiate for some reason or another at some point. Think of all the activities you do on a regular day and try to figure out if you could have gotten away with no negotiation in any of those activities. Like the breakfast you might have to prepare for the family, the simplest of things will require getting the consensus of everyone else. You may argue that that does not happen if you are alone, but you will have to negotiate with yourself on the choices you make for yourself even then.

So, if negotiation is that important in life, why should you not learn to employ the best techniques to negotiate? The power of negotiating gives you the satisfaction of being considered important and gives you self-worth. This is designed to provide you with a set of handy tactics you can use to succeed in your negotiation.

Six Golden Rules for Effective Negotiator

You may believe that the skill of negotiation is something that is innate for some and could be learned by others, but negotiation is not as complex as it seems. It is based on two fundamental aspects, logic and tact. The only problem is that you tend to camouflage these two aspects with all sorts of unwanted behavioral characteristics like ego that completely modifies them out of recognition. You do not want to get into an argument, and neither does anyone else. No one will have negative intentions, and you know that getting yourself into an unwanted scuffle over an issue that can be resolved amicably will only lead to you losing your mental peace. In an attempt to feel you are right or more importantly your opponent is wrong, you tend to forget that it

24

would have been all the better to say, "See, I told you." This is where you need to use negotiation to attain peace and thereby lasting success.

Rule 1 – Identifying Common Ground

First, you need to understand that for a negotiation to occur, you need to find common ground. Take a common situation like a family deciding on a restaurant. Every individual in the family might have a different favorite diner, but their common goal is to have a relaxed meal. Understanding this common goal will reduce sibling rivalry in deciding a feasible dining place that caters to everyone's needs.

To arrive at common ground, you have to think of ways to outline the negotiation so that you can work in partnership to resolve the problem. It's important to remember that your problem is not the person in front of you but the issue in question. You must keep in mind that you do not oppose your opponent, but his stance on the issue. You need to understand that in negotiation, the objective is never to create a winner and a loser but to create a win-win situation for both. You should realize that by wanting to achieve this, you are letting go of that competitive mentality that gives rise to unwanted body language, the undesirable tone in speech, and unwanted words.

This will open doors to realizing the basic goals that you might want to work on in collaboration to meet the common core issue. This will also lead you to be open to others' rationales on the issue and take you forward to the next step proposed by Joseph O'Connor and John Seymour in their book "Stepping Up".

Rule 2 – Stepping Up

The next step in negotiating would be for you to step up. In stepping up, the intention is to identify smaller goals as stepping-stones to achieving a larger goal. For instance, let us say that your ultimate goal is to get an advanced degree in some particular field. You will have to break down your larger goal into smaller, much more manageable goals, such as finding a school whose curriculum and timetables fit your learning requirements and busy schedule.

By stepping up in a negotiation, you see the bigger picture, tend to generalize intentions, and will be able to identify more options in solving the issue than just one non-compromising option. Another benefit of stepping up is that it almost always reminds you that the objective behind the disagreement is not the disagreement at all but is linked to something broader and common to both parties. Therefore, it is very important that when a disagreement arises that you step up before the quarrel evolves, leaving both sides in distress.

Rule 3 – Never Retort

The next technique that you need to keep in mind is never to retort. When an idea is suggested, it means that the person providing the idea had to invest in a lot of thinking before it was suggested. This would mean that they would be highly sensitive to any opposition that is likely to come their way. The best way to negotiate it through would be to give it some time, look at it from their perspective, and consider if the suggested idea has credibility. Instead of disapproving outright, it is better to show them the flaws of their proposal than to tell them. People tend to believe only through personal experience. Later explaining your position will make more sense than it would have, had you retorted in the beginning, and they will automatically see your reasons as to why you disagreed initially.

Rule 4 – Questioning

Questioning the opposition respectfully is the next important step in effective negotiation. If you find a flaw in the person's proposition, then phrase a question which will make the person realize his flaw. Instead of you stating it outright, which will only make the person defensive, intelligent questions are your negotiation weapons which can be used to break down the opposition's proposal in a polite manner while simultaneously leading them towards your idea.

 The best possible manner to put forward a question is to request permission before it, such as "Will you mind answering some questions to satisfy my curiosity?" This will hike up your image and respect in your opposition's eyes, not to mention that you will be guaranteed answers as they cannot elude responding to them once they have given consent.

Rule 5 – Hypothetical Scenario

If nothing seems to be working for you, try guiding the opposition away from the negotiation. You can do this by cleverly changing the discussion tracks towards a hypothetical scenario by using persuasive speech such as "under what circumstances will you consent to my proposition?"

This will corner your opponent into stating the condition(s) which will assure you a successful negotiation, provided you can meet them. If you are a teenager seeking permission from your parents to attend the prom and aren't having any progress convincing them, try asking your parents what they would require from you to consent. This will force them to give you a response, which you can then use to gain what you want.

Rule 6 – Resist Intimation

Learn the art of turning the tables on your opponent. This is necessary only if you are ridiculed for your stance. For instance, if you have proposed an idea that is totally off the wall and inconsistent with the others' suggestions, people will throw sarcastic comments at you to throw you off your feet. The most common phrases you might encounter include "Seriously? You would go ahead with such a plan?", or, "Really? Is that your justification for the whole situation?"

Normally what would happen is that you would try to scrabble together a different, more plausible explanation for your words. Refrain from doing so. Instead, be firm and stand your ground by responding calmly, "Yes, this is all I have to say", or, "Yes, you heard it right; that's my plan." This will throw your audience off their feet and get them scrambling for reasons to try and overthrow your suggestions. If you opt for the former reaction–trying to revise your idea to be more acceptable - you only portray a weak personality and an indecisive mind that will not hold in a negotiation.

Tools for Persuasion

How can you convince people that you are right in your stance? Below are two powerful tactics that you might argue are common habits in conversations yet could be used to steer your client's unconscious mind, spouse, or any opponent to accept your idea without a doubt.

The good option vs. the really bad option

An effective way of putting forward your suggestion would be to exaggerate its benefits in contrast to an amplified negative alternative.

Take the above example of deciding on a place to dine with your family. You might want to eat healthily, so you suggest a vegan restaurant. Your siblings might want to eat junk, so they suggest burgers. Normally you would all shout out your individual choices until you get on your parents' nerves and then end up dining at a totally weird restaurant picked out by your dad.

Here's how you change the scene to your advantage. Remember that the way you frame your suggestion has a profound impact on the outcome of the negotiation. An effective way of putting forward your idea is to compare the available options by portraying your idea as the best option and highlighting the drawbacks of other options. For example, "Do you guys want to eat a wholesome meal at Calorie Counter or eat burgers and increase your chances of developing high cholesterol?"

This puts a spin on the negotiation because it is no longer a negotiation of diners alone, but an option between well-being and bad health choices. Try this tactic once, and you will see how effective it is.

View the available options in terms of hypothetical everyday events.

Compare your options to everyday events in life. This gives context to your negotiation by adding a new simpler dimension to the whole discussion. For example, when you are trying to decide between two dresses, one which costs $100 and another which costs $75, you are most likely to calculate how many days' savings will be invested in this one dress. Another way of looking at it will be to equate the cost to a daily expense of yours, which can be sacrificed for a short while. So instead of looking at the expensive dress as something that will cost you 2 months of saving, try to look at it as taking a tube to work instead of a taxi for one month (the saving will be the cost of your dress).

Similarly, you can use this tactic when trying to persuade someone to buy a costly product, such as a food mixer. Instead of trying to engage in a never-ending bargain with your customers, it would be more effective to equate the product's usefulness to efficiency and time-saving features, which will appeal to clients.

Chapter 6: The Impact of Being in a Manipulative Relationship

Not all trauma causes physical scars. While physical scars can heal, emotional and mental scars run deep. These scars are not always visible, affecting the person for the rest of their life. Mental and emotional manipulation can lead to more problems with trust, intimacy, respect, and safety. If it is not dealt through therapy, the person suffering this trauma may live with this for the rest of their lives.

The short answer is that if any relationship makes you feel worthless, insecure, miserable, depressed, anxious, abused, or any combination of these, you need to get rid of that relationship. Pronto! No one should be the victim of another's agenda. If you've been a victim for far too long, it's time to pull the plug and put a stop to manipulation once and for all. You need to get out as soon as you can. Manipulation is pervasive, and because of that, it can sometimes be difficult to differentiate when a person might be manipulative, and when they might be persuasive. One telltale clue that you could look out for is that there will be a give-and-take, mutually beneficial or constructive relationship dynamic with persuasion. It's time to do some soul searching and seriously ask yourself: Why am I still engaged in this relationship? Why do I have such a hard time walking away?

Short Term Effects of Manipulation

When toxic people have hurt you, it can be difficult to learn to trust again. It is going to take time. The challenge of dealing with toxic people is hard. That is because they have a way of ruining your faith and belief in yourself and other people. To let someone in again and be able to trust them completely, to trust that they are not going to hurt you the way the toxic person did, can be a scary prospect.

Being around manipulators for too long is bound to leave some emotional and mental scars, both long and short term. Recognize that there is a problem. That is how you begin to fix it. To fix and heal yourself from a toxic relationship, you need first to acknowledge that you were in one. You don't have to be embarrassed about it. It's okay to admit that maybe this relationship wasn't the best. Among the short-term side effects of being under the manipulator's thumb for too long, including the following:

- Surprise and Confusion - When it's happening to you, you are confused and surprised that it is happening, and you wonder how someone so close to you can act this way.
- You Question Yourself - You will find yourself questioning yourself -whether you did the right thing, acted the right way, or wrong with you. You go through these mental questions because your manipulator has been questioning everything you do, making your doubt every single move you make.
- Anxiety and Vigilance - You become hypervigilant, sometimes paranoid about yourself and others. You become non-confrontational even when something is wrong, and you need to speak up, become timid although you're being treated unfairly, and not voice your concern.
- Passive - Passiveness becomes you. You feel that taking action leads to more arguments and pain, so your best solution is to be passive by default. This is frequently the

case when someone is in an emotionally abusive relationship.

- Guilt and Shame - You often blame yourself or feel guilty. Your manipulators keep blaming you, and you start believing them, you take it out on yourself and feel even worse.
- No Eye Contact - You eventually stop looking people in the eye. You avoid eye contact and make yourself smaller to take up less space, so you feel you're less likely to be picked on by your manipulator.
- It's Always Walking on Eggshells - You don't know what would cause a meltdown or a spike in their behavior. You start overthinking every step you take to ensure that you don't do things that might anger or upset the manipulator.

Long Term Effects of Manipulation

The truth is, at times we just don't want to believe that someone we know or care about is taking advantage of us. The shock and disbelief lead many people to live in denial about the toxic relationships around them, especially concerning friends and family. Even when there are red flags and warning signs around them, they still find it hard to accept. They may like to make you feel guilty, but don't let the manipulator get inside your head and play on your insecurities by blaming yourself. Self-blame is one of those long-term side effects resulting from being around someone manipulative for far too long. Without therapy or early intervention in getting out of a manipulative relationship, a person may suffer from long-term manipulation consequences.

- Feeling of Numbness and Isolation - You become more and more isolated and numb. From reacting, you become passive, and eventually, you become an observer to the manipulation. You tend to feel nothing at all; you may feel hopeless and damaged and not feel any emotions again.

- Needing Approval - Needing or looking for approval and justification is seen in many different ways. It can be seen as excessively accomplishing a task, being overly nice to everyone, a people pleaser, or being extremely focused on appearance. You tend to feel like you are not enough, and the way to compensate is to make yourself seem flawless and perfect so that other people will appreciate you more.

- Feeling Resentful - Resentment manifests in various ways, primarily irritability, constantly blaming yourself, frustration at not accomplishing a task perfectly, and even impatience. When you have been manipulated for a very long time, it is hard to see anything but bad things yourself.

- Judging Yourself Excessively - You may be holding yourself against very high standards as you feel like you are not good enough. You feel like giving yourself this high standard would make you feel in control. However, this often requires time and self-compassion to move from feeling in control after not being in control for a long time.

- Depressive Disorder and Anxiety - There have been plenty of lies that have been told to you that you believe them yourself over time. All of the above are ways that manipulation can do to oneself, especially over a long period. The great news is that all of these things can be healed. Granted, it can take time, and it is a tough hill to climb, but it is possible.

The process of recovering from manipulation starts with the simple task of appreciating yourself for the way you are. It is imperative to be considerate and kind towards yourself, but you should know that self-love is more than just a sentiment. The healing process is not something that is going to happen overnight. Nor is it something that you can accomplish all in one go. Change can be difficult, so you should do it in small stages. Beyond your capacity to tend to yourself, you must also remember that self-love is an intentional practice and has to be learned and cultivated. It gives you the ability to see yourself completely as yourself and recognize and value your weaknesses, strengths, challenges, and triumphs.

Is It Possible To Heal?

Yes, a resounding YES. Manipulation can be hard to identify, especially when it is among people we are close to. Nobody wants to be labeled as paranoid or crazy because we see and feel things other people don't. Worse still, if someone tells you to 'deal with it' or 'its nature to act that way.' No, it isn't. If you feel manipulated, if you feel wronged, if you feel like you are walking on eggshells all the time, if you feel worried and scared about your every move- that means you are not in a healthy relationship. It doesn't matter if it's with your mom, your dad, your siblings, boyfriend, colleague, manipulators can manifest anywhere.

If you do not detach yourself from manipulative behavior, it can lead to extremely serious mental health problems down the road, leading to depression and anxiety. The time to confront this issue is always now—and here are a few ways to go about the healing process:

- Speak to Yourself - Give yourself a pep talk by asking yourself a few questions. Do you feel like yourself? Do you feel like you are being manipulated? Do you feel unhappy when the person is around? What do you feel when you talk to your manipulator or when they are in the same room? Talking to yourself about these feelings or even writing them down can help you look back and assess things. It can also assure you that you're not the problem. If the same pattern from the manipulator keeps happening the same way in different situations, this is not okay.

- Decide If You Want to Approach the Individual - Keep in mind that this may not be ideal in every situation. Manipulation can happen at work, at home, even in the gym. Depending on your degree of closeness with this person, decide whether it is worth talking to approach them. Sometimes you have no choice but to be around them or work with them. If this is the case, it may help limit your interactions or have someone you trust to be with you when you approach them for their behavior. If you can detach yourself from the situation, such as breaking up with a partner or ending a friendship- do this.

- Talk to People - You are at the center of this healing process. It's about self-love and self-compassion when healing from a manipulative relationship. Talking to someone you trust, someone who understands your position, about how you feel will help you heal. If you can't find someone you are comfortable talking about this with, seek a mental health professional or therapist.

If you can, though, you need to cut off all communication with them. Cut them out of your life for good; your future self will thank you for it. Block their number, delete their social media, ignore their emails and their phone calls. They will try to manipulate you to come back to them by trying to make you feel like they have changed or telling you that they're so sorry and to come back because things are going to be different. When you decide to leave a toxic relationship, it does not mean that you will wake up the next day immediately, feeling like a completely new person. Deciding to leave is just the first step. Healing is a process that takes time. Pain and heartache can be difficult, but these experiences help us grow strong and become better. It teaches us what we want and what we deserve. It sheds light on what you should not put up with and how to live your life to the fullest.

Chapter 7: Media Manipulation: Strategies and How to See Through Them

Some of the tactics and techniques used by various media outlets include psychological manipulation, logical fallacies, rhetorical questions, the use of propaganda, and outright deception. The main focus of this kind of media organization is on suppressing the information and the points of view of the target population while dictating what their options and thoughts should be. Some people will be forced to listen to specific one-sided arguments. People's attention may also be diverted elsewhere, away from the real issues.

There is indeed a huge number of people who may not be aware of "media manipulation." Although people lack basic knowledge about what media manipulation entails, some researchers have taken the bold step to come up with a list of different techniques used by deceptive individuals, such as politicians and media outlets that support them, since they want to control the public.

When looking into different media manipulation techniques, the main focus is on learning more about the techniques used when carrying out mass manipulation. Media manipulation strategies work to ensure that people are submissive, docile, obedient, and don't think for themselves. Additionally, some media outlets can support inequality, capitalism, and neo-capitalism.

Some of the popular media manipulation techniques are as follows:

1. Distraction

The distraction strategy is meant to deviate the target population from focusing on the important issues that pose significance in their lives. To ensure that people are distracted, media houses can flood the news with stories that revolve around trivial issues. The main objective is to ensure that the people are distracted by making sure that their minds are occupied. The result is that people will stop asking why the media is not looking into specific issues. In the process, people will even forget the real issues.

2. Problem-Reaction-Solution

This method can be likened to how politicians try to lure voters during an election period. The population is normally tested first. The first step is to spread rumors, and an evaluation will be carried out to assess how the general population reacts. After creating a problem, the second phase involves offering a solution to the problem. The public will view the manipulators as heroes.

3. Gradualism

This is the process of manipulating people by ensuring that they have accepted some socially unjust decisions. The population is manipulated gradually. The gradual manipulation may take place for many years.

4. Differing

Another strategy used by the media is differing; this is when people present some unpopular decisions, and they may emphasize that the decisions should be implemented since the general population will benefit significantly. The public may believe everything genuinely, and they may make some sacrifices, which they believe will bring forth some significant changes. For instance, the politicians may be the manipulators in this case, and they may trick the voters into thinking that they will lead a better life after the polls. At the end of it all, the people will realize that no changes have been implemented, and they lose faith and disengage from the system.

5. Treating People like Children

The media may be focusing on manipulating the public regularly. When they manipulate the public continuously, it is an indicator that they are treating people like children. The media will try to brainwash people through the use of sugarcoated arguments, intonations, and characters. In turn, the media will assume that people are immature, and they are incapable of handling the truth. The main goal is to ensure that the target audience is docile, submissive, and reacting. Media manipulation ensures that people cannot think like adults.

6. Appealing to People's Emotions

The media has learned more about how to appeal to people's emotions, and their main focus is on ensuring that people are unable to think critically. Various media outlets that want to push an agenda want to control people's thoughts. You should look into how powerful fear is as a tool.

7. Keeping the Public Mediocre and Ignorant

Some media organizations prefer dealing with people who are uncultured and also ignorant. By ensuring that people are isolated from various pieces of knowledge, the media can easily manipulate the public, which is also true for certain politicians. The media also ensures that a rebellion does not take place since people are ignorant.

8. Encouraging the Public to Accept Mediocrity

Ensuring that the public accepts mediocrity is similar to ensuring that the general population is ignorant. The media prefers to make use of such strategies when manipulating people. For instance, is the media airing the shows that people want to watch? Are some shows imposed on us by the media? In short, do we get to consume the content that we want, or does the media impose different pieces of content on us? At times it is clear that the media is brainwashing us, and we have ceased to care much about our surroundings. Also, we have been trained to be mediocre.

9. Self-Blame

The media usually encourages self-blame and ignorance and makes sure that people believe that they are responsible for their misfortunes. In short, the media will focus on self-incrimination and will make sure that the public will not mobilize at all costs.

10.   Completing the Knowledge of the Public

To control the general public, the media has focused on learning more about its audience. The media can work together with other companies to learn more about every individual to manipulate the masses easily.

It is advisable to learn more about how to spot media manipulation. The resources talking about how to spot media manipulation are few; thus, we cannot delve into the topic in an in-depth manner. However, pay attention, and you may notice now when various media outlets are trying to manipulate people.

Chapter 8: Why Self-Discipline And Self-Control Are Important?

Relationship Among Self-Control, Self-Discipline, And Willpower

Willpower is your inner strength to take action, decision, and execute any task until it is done regardless of your outer and inner resistance, difficulties and discomfort. It helps you overcome temptations, negative habits, and laziness and carry different actions even though it requires effort and unpleasant experiences.

Self-discipline is the rejection of your instant gratification to achieve something better or to achieve a better goal. A person also can stick with thoughts, actions and behavior which can lead to success and improvement. Self-discipline is also self-control which can be manifested in physical, emotional, spiritual and mental discipline. However, self-discipline is not living in a restrictive or limiting lifestyle. It is also not being narrow-minded. Self-discipline and self-control is one of the pillars of willpower and success.

You need self-control and self-discipline to make daily decisions and actions. You also need it in making important decisions and reaching major achievements in life. Self-discipline and self-control are needed to continue studying, start a business, lose weight, maintain long-lasting relationships, change habits, meditate, have self-improvement, and keep promises.

Willpower, Discipline, Self-Control

• Developing mental strength

Every tip given till now, every piece of advice, links back to using your mental prowess to overcome sloth. The unfortunate part is that everyone wants to be productive and successful. Still, very few want to invest in developing a strong mind – with which they can control their destinies.

What's mental strength? Your mind can listen to you in the face of temptation or inaction. And it's a combination of your willpower and self-control, tempered by discipline. Indeed, the first two are almost synonyms of each other, while the third is the outcome. It can be safely said any one of them is incomplete without the other two.

Let's understand these attributes in detail.

Defining Willpower

Willpower is considered as the ability to overcome instant pleasure, and resist temptation in the short term to achieve goals in the long term. Most of us have heard of the 'marshmallow experiment' in which a kid is left in a room with a single marshmallow for an hour. If he resists the temptation to eat it in that time, he gets two marshmallows later. More kids waited for the second marshmallow than settle for just one.

Strong willpower helps you overpower feelings and emotions while empowering you to ride through logic. Many individuals develop it consciously as a tool to regulate their actions. Psychologists contend that willpower is a limited resource, to be used carefully. However, this premise hasn't been corroborated by research yet.

Willpower is the force that gives you self-control, with which you can avoid succumbing to momentary impulses. It empowers us to pause and think – so that you can look at optional responses. It also prevents you from jumping into things that could be regrettable later.

Scientifically speaking, willpower resides in the right brain in a section called prefrontal cortex. Willpower is known to use up glucose, causing depletion of the ego. When this happens, our reserves are low and our guard is down, and we tend to indulge and overeat. This explains why people going through stress tend to put on weight easily.

In layman's terms, willpower can do something even if you don't feel like doing it. Research studies have shown that kids who grow up with more self-control become adults who're stable and secure, not to mention scoring high in self-discipline. This, in turn, leads to better performance academically and happier lives. Self-control is the one single contributor to the long-term success of an individual.

Willpower is like brainpower. Use it less and it weakens. Employ it more and more and it gets fitter and stronger. If you've always lived a life of surrender, it would be tough for you to develop willpower. Some psychologists also liken it to a muscle – neglect using it and it sags. Keep stretching it and it gets more resilient.

Needless to add, self-control is the key to overcome fears and obsessions, and to prevent unwelcome behavioral traits. When practiced well, it puts you in charge of your life, developing your tolerance and patience, improving your relationships, and repeatedly succeeding. It also empowers you to avoid excesses and attain moderation; assists you control your moods and reject negativity; and strengthens your self-esteem and inner strength. Self-control helps you to become a complete, well-rounded personality.

But for willpower to work, you need to make it work – and you should be determined for it. Temptation appeals to the subconscious while willpower resides in the conscious, so you need to make constant, serious efforts to improve it. Here are few simple ways to add more muscle to your will.

Try To Resist Temptation At Every Opportunity

We've all heard the cliché: 'Where there's a will, there's a way.' Temptation is all around us – in different sizes, shapes and intensities. From enjoying a cake to watching a thriller, everything is temptation. When faced with one, attempt to ward it off. Tell your mind to fight it and immerse yourself in some other activity. It may not work the first time, or even the second, but gradually you'll gain the strength to fight it. Just say No and stay with your decision.

If At First You Don't Succeed, Postpone

This works like magic. If you can't say No to the cake right away, tell yourself that you'll have it tomorrow. When tomorrow comes, say the same thing. Keep putting it off, and eventually you'll realize that you're not tempted by it anymore. This is because your mind can't accept No for an answer. But if you tell your mind that you can have it later, it agrees. Postpone temptation forever.

Point to remember: Don't tire your will by constant negation. If you constantly deny it the pleasure it's seeking, its edge gets blunted. Since willpower isn't considered to be infinite you've got to expend it with care. Hence the next point.

Remove All Temptations From Your Vicinity

If cakes are your weakness don't store them in your refrigerator. Prevent temptations from entering your home, then there's no way you'll fall for them. If the television is a temptation, unplug it or – better still – disconnect the cable connection. Out of sight is out of mind, and you don't miss what you don't see (in most cases). Guarantee that your immediate environment is free from such attractions; your willpower will thank you for it.

Equip Your Body To Resist Temptation

If you're serious about boosting your willpower, you need to get your body prepared. See that you eat nutritious food, get enough exercise and sleep well. Regular workouts help you to fight stress better, leading to better self-control. And the good news is, you don't have to spend hours in the gym every day. Even light exercise like taking a walk or doing basic yoga can enhance your resilience.

Make Affirmations Work For You

Self-affirmations can lead to better self-control. When your affirmations are positive and confident, and repeated often, they have a lasting impact on your mind. There's a world of difference between "I can't have that cheese pizza" instead of "I don't want to have that cheese pizza". The former suggests your limitation while that latter indicates confidence.

Whenever you feel the need to boost your self-control, say these affirmations over and over again:

- I am in full control of myself.
- I am in full control of my reactions to external stimuli.
- I am in full control of my behavior.
- I am the master of my life.
- I possess the power to choose my thoughts and emotions.

- I understand that my self-control gives me inner strength.
- I am, with each passing day, enhancing my abilities to control myself.
- I practice self-control because it's a lot of fun.

Simple Self-Discipline Workouts

We refuse to do several things in our everyday life, purely because we lack the mental strength to do them. These could be small acts, seemingly insignificant, but with the potency to enhance our inner muscle and make us better individuals. We hesitate to do them for a variety of reasons, including laziness, low confidence and self-esteem, low mental strength, shy and ,timid or plain procrastination. A part of us may want to do it, but we stagger and lose the opportunity, only to regret it later. This is where our mind plays a role in increasing our willpower.

- Your sink is full of dirty dishes and you're surfing the Internet mindlessly. Force yourself to reach for the Shut Down button, close the computer, and head towards the sink. Don't fall for any more procrastination. Start with cleaning just one spoon and soon you'll find yourself cleaning up the entire sink. It's your win against your sloth.
- A pregnant woman enters the subway carriage and no seat is empty. You have the choice to give her your seat but you hesitate. Don't. Do it for yourself, not for her or for the sake of being nice. Give her the seat and record a minor victory.
- You come back home from a tired day outdoors. You know you need to wash. But your mind tells you that you're fatigued beyond repair, so you just sit in front of the television watching senseless stuff. Don't believe

yourself. Don't let yourself be taken for a ride. You do have the strength to walk into the shower and bathe. You'll feel so fresh that you'll be glad you did. More importantly, you would have triumphed over yourself.

Look around and find dozens of similar instances where you're offered a choice – one, the usual easy route and the other, the unusual difficult one. Choose the difficult route always. Take the stairs instead of the elevator, walk instead of seeking a lift, hit the gym instead of sleeping early in the morning. Each such act of yours strengthens your willpower a little more. Become a strong personality, not a weakling at the mercy of your faint heart. Conquer yourself and you can defeat the world.

Solutions Snapshot

Develop mental strength through willpower, self-control and discipline.

A strong willpower is behind self-control.

Willpower is like muscle; its strength can be enhanced through practice.

There are many benefits of willpower. It helps you become happy and successful.

Have the will to make willpower work. Here are some tips:

- Attempt to resist temptation at every step.
- If you can't say No right now, postpone yielding to temptation.
- Remove all enticements from around you. Out of sight, out of mind.
- Eat healthy food, get exercise, sleep well – all help fight temptation.

- Use self-affirmation to develop inner strength.
- Test your mental prowess during simple everyday events.
- You can't conquer the world if you fail to conquer yourself.

Chapter 9:   The Sustainability Of An Excellent Emotional State Of Mind

We will now discuss a fundamental concept for all the thoughts and ideas that you have learned. An attempt to completely change the anxiety narrative and present a complete solution-driven model that will help you overcome emotional issues permanently all relies on one word—sustainability!

It is so inspiring to learn new ideas about the steps you can take toward better anxiety management, but what is better than learning is the idea of sustaining what you learn. Anxiety is a feeling, and like all other feelings, it can creep up on you at any time even when you seem to know what to do.

So the best approach to imbibe is the sustainability approach that enables you to make the lessons gained a vital part of your life. With the sustainability approach, you will be taking decisive steps that will help you go beyond wanting to change negative thoughts to positive ones and just being 100% positive all the time.

Yes, it is possible to have positive thoughts all the time. It requires a lot of work, commitment, intentionality, and dedication to the process; but it is possible.

Emotional Resilience

For you to sustain the answers, you've discovered that you will need to be emotionally resilient. Resilience is like a muscle. You've got to flex it enough to so it can take on more emotional punches. Resilience isn't about winning the battle of emotions; it is about the strength you display every time you are faced with an issue.

Some persons discover answers to their anxiety; they apply the solutions and erroneously believe that they wouldn't have any other issue going forward. So when they are hit by something more significant than the initial anxiety, they buckle under and fall into the pit of depression.

But an emotionally resilient person doesn't give up. They are aware of the repetitive cycle of emotions and are prepared to take it on at any time, regardless of how hard it might be.

Listen, regardless of what you've learned, there will be moments when you feel like you haven't learned anything at all; and in those pivotal points, what you need is emotional resilience. You will need the kind of emotional toughness that will cause you to strive on and maintain a positive outlook about life.

Emotional resilience also helps you bounce back from stressful situations that may have otherwise held you down and become worse. Resilience is not an "I can bend but not break" trait; instead, it is an "I know I am broken, but I can pull myself back together again."

When you are emotionally resilient, you do not only adapt quickly to stress, negative emotions, or disappointment but also gain insight into some of the best ways you can avoid the kind of situations that lead you right back to that emotional space.

So how can you build emotional resilience?

First, you must be self-aware, which is the ability to stay in tune with your feelings. This will help you avoid the pitfall of blaming the world for your challenges. Instead, you will learn how to look within for answers. You can also build emotional resilience by being persistent. You develop that never-giving-up attribute, which keeps your internal motivation alive.

Emotional control is another way of ensuring that you've got emotional resilience. When you think carefully before making a decision, you will most likely protect yourself from many issues later.

Emotionally resilient individuals are also very flexible with their thinking patterns. They have a mix of rationality, positive thinking, and adjustability, all essential parts of positive mental health.

The attributes will help you build emotional resilience, which will be instrumental in the sustenance of a positive mindset. If you aren't emotionally tough, you will have many moments where you break down and stay down (which is the lowest form of the impact of anxiety).

We are saying here that it is okay to fall, but don't stay down. When you build emotional resilience using the ideas provided thus far, you will be able to get over negative emotional situations and build yourself strong enough to inspire others going through a similar challenge.

Have A Support System

Emotional resilience is crucial, and in addition to that, you must have a great support system around you. We all need support, especially when dealing with sensitive issues, but we will enjoy the best kind of support from people who genuinely care about us.

When you feel overwhelmed, sometimes you may not be able to do anything to help yourself at that particular moment. This happens when you are dealing with something very painful or an event that has such a huge effect on your emotions.

What you need at such times is to rely on someone else who will help make the emotional burden light. You may need a hug, a smile, or someone to talk to, regardless of what you need. Support systems are essential to helping you sustain a positive mindset.

Most people do not get to bask in the feeling of having support systems because they don't share their challenges, and when they are asked if they are all right, they go with the natural response, "I am fine."

When dealing with anxiety, it isn't the time to lie to yourself or others. If you do have people who love and care for you, that is an added advantage you must utilize to solidify your built mindset.

Well, now is the time to put that lesson to good use by not only being expressive to yourself but being expressive with others who may be able to help you through moments of mental crisis.

There is an erroneous belief adopted by many persons that states that if you share your struggles with others, you will become vulnerable, and they may take advantage of you. Well, the reason this idea is erroneous is that if you are with people that love you, then you wouldn't worry about someone taking advantage of you.

Do not allow the statements made by other people to shut yourself off from others. You've got to open yourself to sharing so that you can derive joy in great company.

Sometimes when you share, you don't need advice. You might only need to get some things off your mind, and you are bound to feel better afterward. Try not to isolate yourself from others. You never know who might become that accountability partner that will pick your telephone call in the middle of the night when faced with an emotional crisis.

Your support system may include very close friends, family members, or your romantic partner. Some people join emotional support groups that consist of people dealing with anxiety, and they come together to help one another. If you've got the right people around you for support, then great. You can also join a support group if you feel reluctant to share the details of your anxiety to those dearest to you.

We are building a sustainable pattern with the solutions we have offered, and support systems are a part of that pattern. If everyone has people in our lives, we can lean on; the world will surely be a better place for it. There will be fewer cases of people who feel alone with their challenges and more success stories of people who come together and stay connected over a common goal, eradicating adverse emotional problems.

Reach Out To Someone Else

When you have a great support system and the right mental tools to beat anxiety, what can you do to make it all better? Reach out and help someone else who may be unable to get out of that place. Listen, the best way to become extremely good at something is to share in the experience with someone else.

Some people are going through this challenge and have no one to hold their hands. There is little or no hope for such individuals, and you can contribute in your way to make it better. Now you may not be able to reach out to many people, but you can reach out to those within your sphere of contact.

Use all the ideas you've discovered and the ideas that have worked for you on this journey to help someone else. You wouldn't know someone is dealing with anxiety by just waiting for them to burst into tears or have a moody look. You need to interact with people on a deeper level. Ask questions and remain connected with them before some of them open up to you.

When you help others, you will also be solidifying the solutions you've imbibed because you will be required to do some of the solution-driven activities with these people you help. As you improve on your emotional strength, the people you help will lean more on you and get better.

Anxiety is a demoralizing challenge for anyone to go through, but what makes it better is knowing that you've got someone with you through it all and deriving motivation from that person.

When we speak of volunteering and helping those on the streets, everyone (the rich and middle class) is often encouraged to participate; they are often told to give willingly regardless of how small their gifts are. Well, it is the same with helping someone who struggles with anxiety. You don't have to become an expert on dealing with stress before reaching out.

Sometimes it might be a visit you pay to the person's home to listen to them; it might be a hug, a gift of this book, or a kind smile to a stranger. There are countless ways of reaching out to another person; you need first to become sensitive to others and try to see their pain beneath the smiles and pretense at being "fine."

Be very patient with the people around you. Some people may not be willing to share their challenges with you even if they believe you can help. You have a responsibility to persist respectfully and be a shoulder for them to lean on. Helping others also makes it possible for you to look beyond yourself and seek ways to make positive contributions to the world in your small way.

You don't have to start out helping a lot of people at once. Start with one person. Succeed with the individual. Ensure thorough feedback. Then reach out to someone else. Being charitable with your time and emotional effort will cause you to become increasingly conscious of your own emotions and others. You will be able to perform the dual function of being a caregiver to yourself and other people.

Don't just read through this book, then put it down, and forget to use the content to impact others. You can be an agent of change in the world today in your unique way.

Chapter 10:   Embracing Our Feelings

Feeling An Emotion

To change the difficult behaviors that occur when we are emotionally reactive. It is necessary to replace the behaviors with new and more functional one. This may result in an increased awareness of our feelings. Habitual behaviors serve to take our attention away from underlying feelings that seem overwhelming. When these behaviors stop, the smoke clears and the underlying feelings become more apparent to us.

To handle the feeling component of an emotion, take the opposite approach. Instead of stopping the feeling, allow it. Instead of changing the feeling to something more positive, embrace it as it is.

The healthy response to feeling is not changing it, moving away from it, or distracting attention from it. Instead, embrace the feeling with awareness. Feeling is a natural response of our bodies to a situation or how we perceive that situation. Problems that we have with our emotions lie in distorted perceptions, not in feelings. Feelings demand to be fully felt. If we push the feeling away, we replace it with numbness and repression or self-destructive actions that distract from feelings. Avoidance of feelings is the source of painful symptoms and defenses. This is why it is so important to embrace feelings, even when we are being emotionally reactive.

Many people run away when confronted with uncomfortable feelings. They are unpleasant; they seem negative. To embrace them is like doing a 180-degree turn. Why embrace unpleasant feelings--like the feelings that accompany emotional reactivity? It is important to understand that they are not destructive. Rather, the behaviors that are used to avoid these feelings are the destructive element. For instance, a person may feel sadness over the loss of a friend, and instead of feeling the sadness will drown his sorrows in drink. In this scenario, drinking is destructive. Embracing the feelings of grief, however, will eventually lead to their transformation.

Throughout a lifetime we develop numerous, unconscious methods to avoid painful feelings. By embracing our feelings, the compulsion to act these strategies out is short-circuited, and we take the wind out of the sails of defensiveness. If one's tendency is to avoid feelings of hurt by becoming angry, once that hurt is embraced and allowed, then the strategy of avoiding hurt by getting angry has no more purpose. The underlying pain and hurt is faced and transformed.

Painful feelings often become associated with painful events. We believe that if we allow the feelings to arise, we will be vulnerable and hurt again. But the feelings we experience now are not those of past experiences. They are merely changes in our physiology and are not necessarily harmful. What is harmful is running away from our feelings. By embracing painful feelings instead of pushing them away, we can heal.

A feeling is made up of sensations in our bodies as nerve cells become activated. Blood flow changes, adrenaline increases and other chemical changes occur when we are emotional. Feeling is the awareness of these many sensations being stimulated and an evaluation of pleasantness, unpleasantness or neutrality. Negative feelings in themselves cannot be horrible or overwhelming, only unpleasant. The true negativity resides in our beliefs and thoughts about them. Understanding this can be a powerful reminder that feelings are okay and are not monsters to be avoided.

Learning To Soothe Ourselves

One analogy we can use is comparing our emotions to an infant's responses because infants are highly emotional and have not yet developed the defenses or intellects of adults. They are very sensitive on a feeling level. When an infant is upset and runs to her mother, the mother needs only to hold the infant and attend to her to calm the infant's high emotional arousal. Being held by a loving caregiver creates a situation where the original emotion changes, sometimes to its opposite. The child may be laughing and smiling within a few minutes. Feelings require similar attention. We need to soothe ourselves by holding the feeling and staying with it until it changes - until we feel soothed and calmed down.

The ability to soothe ourselves emotionally is a principal skill in mastering emotions. We learn this from our caregivers when we are infants. Those unable to soothe themselves may experience distressing emotions for longer periods. Often dysfunctional behaviors serve as distractions from these uncomfortable feeling states. By learning to embrace the feeling component of our emotions and soothe ourselves, the impetus for these negative behaviors decreases dramatically. The troublesome behaviors may remain a habit, but the compulsion to act them out loses much of its power.

It is of primary importance that we change our view of our emotions. We need to stop trying to change them or avoid them, instead, let them come to full awareness. If we can make this discovery — that feelings are our friends and have important information for us — we can build the necessary skills to master our emotions and reactivity.

Steps For Embracing Our Feelings

1. Move your attention to the feeling rather than away from it.
2. Bring your awareness fully to the feeling without backing away or getting distracted. Stay with the feeling.
3. Explore the feeling. What does it feel like? Are there images that occur to you as you explore the feeling? Note the images but keep your attention on the feeling.
4. Notice the specific parts of your body that are affected by the feeling. Where in your body are you feeling this? See if you can break the feeling down into its parts. Notice what specific sensations are in your body.
5. Let your breathing relax. Take a deep breath. As you do this, imagine that you are breathing directly into the area where you are feeling the emotion.
6. Be aware if the feeling changes, and notice its energetic quality. Whether the feeling is anger or sadness, it is just energy. Stay with the feeling and see what changes take place.
7. This exercise should be soothing. If it is not, some fears or memories hold this feeling in place and not allow it to move.

By staying with the feeling and experiencing it in our bodies, we contain it and own it. It does not own us. Knowing that feelings are sensations in our bodies allows us to form a container around them. Awareness is the container that surrounds the emotion and it is larger than the emotion. Awareness contains everything that we are experiencing in the moment: sights, sounds, thoughts, sensations in our bodies. We may be feeling extreme anger in every cell of our bodies, yet our awareness is greater. We can see the trees and the sky, and they have nothing to do with our anger. Instead of seeing anger as a force that sweeps us away, reduce the anger to its true size. Notice how the emotion appears in your body whenever a strong emotion occurs.

As we learn to embrace and experience feeling, a significant transformation takes place--the feelings change. Our feelings have one basic need — to be felt. When we receive this message, it fulfills its task. The feeling may then move to calmness or some other more positive emotion as long as there is no distorted thinking to support its continuance.

Another thing that takes place as we embrace feeling is a change in our deep belief structure. Negative beliefs about experiencing intense feelings fade. We realize that we have embraced the most intense feelings. Yet, nothing horrible has happened to us, which helps us break the deep associative ties between these feelings and previous experiences of abuse and distress. We learn that by feeling the feelings, we may soothe ourselves and calm ourselves down. Embracing our feelings now leads to a positive and healing outcome. This is a key method of healing faulty emotional learning during abusive situations and comes to the surface when we are emotionally reactive.

Numbness And Embracing Feelings

As cited earlier, there are three basic ways of expressing emotional reactivity: conflict, caretaking and avoidance. All three of these methods avoid feelings to some extent. Let's explore how avoiders can come into greater contact with their emotions.

The avoidant style can be so pervasive for some that it becomes part of their personality style. Because it is difficult for them to experience strong emotions, they avoid them altogether and rarely allow themselves to feel. It may appear that they are not emotionally reactive because they seem calm and peaceful. Still, this calmness is due to avoiding situations that trigger their emotions rather than true peace of mind. They are engaged in a pre-emptive strike; their avoidant behavior itself is their emotional reactivity.

The avoidant person needs to learn to identify avoidant behaviors and to stop them. Awareness of these behaviors is difficult because the rationalizations behind them are so complete. The individual engages in excuse-making, judgments, and other defense mechanisms to justify avoidance and disguise it. A person may even get so far away from his emotions that he no longer feels them, even in situations that would typically trigger intense emotions. Some people talk about serious abuse in their childhood as if they were reporting on someone else's childhood. Sometimes a person may express bizarre behaviors, such as laughing when describing how they were physically abused as children. This dissociation from one's feelings occurs in many people who have had overwhelming trauma.

Chapter 11:   Reflect On The Bright Side Of Life Everyday

You Can't Change The Past Or Predict The Future: Live In The Present

Living in the present can be a difficult feat to achieve for many. Whether it is through their upbringing or as a result of various environmental factors, most people have been conditioned to dwell about the past and to worry about the future. Even today's technology contributes to one's inability to focus on the present.

Take, for example, the notifications you receive from your phone. You may be fully engrossed in whatever you are doing at the moment. Still, when you hear your phone go off, the mind tends to automatically switch to either an experience or a future event related to the notification you have received.

Other factors that can keep you from staying in the present include:

·   the natural tendency of the mind to edit out the positive aspects of your previous experiences, thus making the past seem more negative than it was; and

·   the uncertainty of the current situation you are in, which generates feelings of anxiety, negative thoughts, and worry.

Many people find it difficult to overcome these elements and start living in the present. Some do not even know what it means to be in the present. They cannot imagine how it feels like to be free from their ruminations about the past, and their apprehensions about the future. Most of the time, they simply do not have enough personal will to focus on what is currently happening to them.

Fortunately, there are various ways to get over the challenges of being in the here and now. Through the right mindset and a positive attitude, you can start living in the present and make better life choices.

When you live in acceptance of what has already happened, and what will come to pass, then you will begin seeing things for what they truly are. You will be able to forgive yourself and others for the mistakes that have been made in the past. You will also be able to free yourself from feelings of anxiety and worry about the things that may come your way.

Let me share my personal experience on this subject!

So, it just happens that I had made at some point in my life, quite too many financial mistakes and bad financial investments that did cost me some huge chunk of my savings for the supposed pleasant life I looked forward to living. Not once, not twice, not even thrice. Under these circumstances, I should have typically read the signs on the wall, right? and know what investment is good and bad, but duh! (laughs), I kept sinking in much money in more investments, but this time around, to recover my previous financial losses. However, I ended up losing more and more. At a point, I lost it and went into bouts of anxiety, negative thoughts, and worries about the mess I created in my finances and how I should have known better after the initial three losses incurred. I would overthink what would become of my financial status, especially at the point of my life where I was somewhat out of a job. I was scared, unhappy, and angry every other day I lived. This feeling went on for as long as I could remember, and then, on one Tuesday morning, I laid woken right on my bed and looked up, gazing into the ceiling before me, and I asked myself, a life-changing question.

"How has my overthinking of the past financial mistakes, what I could have done differently, and what the life I hoped to live in the future has helped me achieve?".

I decided that I was going to leave the past mistakes where it belongs, "the past"— I was going to focus on living in the present by making the most out of it— and that I wasn't going to beat myself up about what the future holds. Consciously deciding on this gave me a great sense of relief and peace.

No matter how much we try, we can't change the past simply because it is out of our control, and no matter how we wish we could predict the future, we simply can't because the universe operates on its terms and conditions. So then, the obvious choice you can make, one which you have control of is to live in the moment and enjoy what each day brings. It sure helps.

Change The Way You Think: Gratitude Vs. Regret

Everyone has felt regret at different points in life. You may have gotten over them by now, but you have surely experienced how heavy regrets can be.

Regret can be something you have done—whether deliberately or unintentionally—to hurt yourself or somebody else. You may also regret after making a snap decision that resulted in something less favorable than it should have been had you only taken your time.

Having regrets is a normal human experience. However, obsessing over them is not healthy or productive, and would most likely result to overthinking, which in turn would produce bouts of anxiety, negative thoughts, and worry. There is no way to go back in time and change the circumstances that have led to those regrets. The only way to go is forward.

To overcome a regretful mindset, you must learn how to adapt and apply gratitude in your life. Rather than ruminating about what has happened and what could have been, you should switch your attention to the good things in your life.

Changing the way you think is not something you can do half-heartedly. You must learn how to practice gratitude whichever way you can. You can do it by literally keeping track of the fortunate instances you have experienced in life. Others find the habit of writing down positive things to help keep them grateful, especially during tough times.

You can even take this further by being thankful for the lessons you have gained from your past, no matter how painful or hard they are. Be thankful that you have managed to live through them, and you have then been allowed to learn from your past mistakes. You are now a step closer to enlightenment and becoming a better version of you.

Once you have chosen to adopt a grateful mindset fully, then you will be able to:

- feel contentment about the blessings in your life;
- gain an optimistic point of view;
- better appreciate the people around you;
- find ways to help those in need; and
- have a higher level of self-awareness.

Take note that successfully overcoming your regrets does not happen overnight. You must be patient with yourself, and continually practice applying gratitude in all aspects of your life.

The more you practice it, the easier it becomes to access a grateful mindset, even during trying times.

Act With Confidence: Stop Asking "What If"?

Torturing yourself with the question "what if" gives you nothing but unnecessary feelings of anxiety, negative thoughts, and worry. There is no way to know what will exactly happen by choosing to act in a certain way. It is a waste of time and energy to think about the uncontrollable aspects of the future.

More often than not, obsessing over your actions' possible outcomes will only make you feel upset. Having no definite answer since there is an endless number of possibilities can be particularly unsettling.

To stop asking yourself this question, you must:

- focus on the here and now of the situation;
- identify the things that are within your control; and
- think of each situation as an opportunity to learn.

If you do end up acting upon the wrong decision, the only healthy thing to do is learn from it and move on. Do not let your mistake define your present and what your future would become.

Reallocate the time and energy you would have used in overthinking about the what-ifs of the situation into something more productive. Use that as a motivation to make better decisions the next time you are facing a similar circumstance. Remember, you can take more control over your thoughts and actions if you simply believe you can do so.

Do Away With Negativity And Embrace Positivity

There are days when nothing seems to go your way. The moment you wake up, you just know everything that can go wrong will go wrong.

Since you are already expecting it, any disappointment that comes your way further strengthens the negative vibes you feel. When this happens over and over again, those vibes solidify into a perennial negative mindset.

If this scenario sounds familiar to you, then know that you have the option to turn things around for the better. You are in control, and you can choose how you will approach important matters in your life.

From here, you can start nurturing a positive mindset centered around your personal growth and development. You can reframe your outlook in life, thus giving you hope and motivation to overcome the challenges that may come your way.

It should be noted that you should actively work on embracing positivity. Once you have acknowledged that you have the right to be happy and ultimately responsible for your happiness, you may then apply this positive mindset in your day-to-day life and the achievement of your goals.

Chapter 12: Ways To Attract Good Energy

Positive energy can improve how we feel and communicate with the people around us. In our daily dealings with other people, we receive the kind of energy we send out. This energy is usually within our entire body, spirit and mind and, when it vibrates out, it's usually felt by others around us.

The way we feel about the people around us results from the kind of energy we carry around and the energy that we pick up on from them. We may feel free and cheerful around some people and feel awkward and cold when we're around other people. Maintaining positive energy will improve our total well-being and help us to communicate more positively with people.

On the other hand, negative energy negatively affects our entire well-being due to the feelings of resentment, discord and unhappiness that accompany it. So, your ultimate goal should be to resist negative energy and embrace positive energy.

You can achieve this by increasing your energy level and surrounding yourself with positivity. Here are nine daily ways to boost your inner vibration and help you feel the energy flow around you.

Pay Attention To The Energy You Release

If you're releasing lots of negative energy, there's no way you'll attract positive energy. How others feel when they are with you tells a lot about the kind of energy you discharge. Do people feel calm and happy or gloomy and sad when they're with you? Your answer to this will help you know if you have to work on boosting your energy or not.

Negative energy will always impact your relationships negatively, and your attitude towards others is a reflection of who you are. Ask yourself: What kind of impression do I make on people?

If you're the type that always reaches out to people and creates great relationships, you may be releasing positive energy. If you're the type that people avoid, you may be releasing negative energy. Therefore, you must focus on emitting positive energy.

Change The Way You Think

If you spend most of your time thinking about negativity, you'll become a pessimist in no time. But if you spend most of your time thinking about the positive aspects of your life, no matter how hard that can sometimes be, you'll easily attract good things. Always ensure that the positive thoughts guide you in all you do.

If you're battling a bad situation, resist the urge to slip into pessimism. Instead, tell yourself that it's only a phase, and it will soon pass. Always engage in positive affirmations, especially when things go wrong. When you receive bad news, try not to dwell on it or catastrophize. Replace negative thoughts with positive ones. Let the inspiration for your actions come from positive and realistic thoughts about yourself.

Discard Negative Influences

Quit surrounding yourself with negative people, things or places will take away your happiness and total well-being. Some people are toxic, and you should be far away from them. These are people who always try to discourage you from everything you do and look for every means to bring you down constantly. If you're not observant enough, you may begin to pick up bad habits from these toxic places, people or things.

When you disengage yourself from these negative influences, you'll be able to design the kind of life you want for yourself. At times, disentangling from these influences may seem difficult because they're a part of your daily life. If this is the case, avoid them at all costs and prepare yourself mentally if you cannot avoid running into them.

Increase Your Circle

As you discard negative influences, increase your circle of positive influences. Surround yourself with people of like minds that can influence you positively and inspire you to be the best you can be. Ensure that you hold these relationships in high esteem and nurture them.

These people should be able to be honest and authentic with you, but it shouldn't be done to spite you or make you feel less sure of yourself. The positive energy that radiates from this group will help you live a happier life.

Be Kind And Compassionate

Some little acts of kindness can have a significant impact on the receiver and the giver. Being kind and compassionate towards others has been proven to attract lots of positivity and good relationships. So, the more you give and show compassion to others, the better your physical and mental well-being will be.

Being kind is also a great way to motivate the people around you and inspire them to be kind to others. Smiling to people around you, serving someone a cup of tea or doing anything that makes people around you happy sends loads of positive energy to you, which boosts your inner happiness.

Be Grateful

Each day, if you dwell too much on negative thoughts, you'll find it hard to see the things you ought to be grateful for. Devote most of your quiet time to thinking about the little things in your life and be thankful for them. Doing this will help you let go of harmful and toxic emotions.

Think of the good things and people in your life and why you are grateful for them. Doing this for a few minutes every day will help you a great deal. If you can't think of any right now, you can begin by keeping a gratitude journal and jotting down a list of things that make you happy and feel contented. Being grateful will help you reflect on the bad times you've had and how you overcame them all.

Discover Your Inner Strength

Taking your focus away from all the negative thinking that may erode your confidence level and cause feelings of insecurity and self-doubt and shifting to positive thinking that boosts your self-esteem and confidence is essential to developing inner strength. Inner strength is what will make you resilient in the face of stressful situations and help boost your energy level so that you can handle whatever comes your way.

Align Your Current Self With Your Future Self

The things you spend your time and money on will determine how far you'll go in life. These choices you make today will shape your life tomorrow. Ask yourself: What do I desire most in the world? Work towards being the person that your future self will be proud of by building healthy relationships and a healthy lifestyle.

Develop a picture in your mind of who you would like to be in the future and start taking steps to make it a reality. Doing this will help you exert more control over your life, and the more positive actions you take, the more positive the reality you will create for your future self.

Act In Good Faith

There's a general belief in business that both parties act in good faith as they work together. We all benefit from treating one another fairly, but only a few people understand that this principle should be followed as we interact daily personally or professionally.

Endeavour to be nice to everyone you meet and treat them with respect, and in most cases, you'll receive the same gesture. Even if someone wrongs to you, avoid retaliation as it won't make you feel better. They may be having a bad day and react negatively to you for this reason. So, when you act nicely to everyone, even when they react harshly to you, you can be sure to attract positive energy, and this will help a lot.

Chapter 13:   Daily   Emotional Management Rituals

To truly master your emotions, you will need to go a lot further than just engaging in sporadic emotional management practices, anytime emotion is triggered within you. You will need to be willing to intentionally work with your emotions every day so that you can acknowledge, process, and release your emotions on a day-to-day basis. In doing so, you are allowing yourself to release your emotional reserves to not hold onto them longer than necessary. You also allow yourself to create space for you to learn from your emotions and discover new ways to deal with them more healthily and productively. As you will discover over time, your emotions are something that you will continually learn from every single day. The process of learning how to navigate emotions healthily and productively is one that lasts a lifetime, largely because every time an emotion is triggered, it will be under different circumstances. The more emotion is triggered, especially under different circumstances, the more you become aware of how those emotions feel for you, and how you can navigate those emotions more effectively.

There are many ways that you can create a daily emotional management ritual for yourself, with no one answer being right or wrong. The key to finding a ritual that works best for you is to identify what your life tends to look like from an emotional point of view and to create a ritual that works best for you. An ideal ritual should address how you feel and help you learn from and release those emotions all at once. If you are dealing with a particularly troubling emotion, your daily ritual should include some form of activity intended for helping you process that emotion, too. This way, you are always working within your needs and supporting your overall and day-to-day emotional wellbeing.

Stay Committed to Your Daily Mindfulness Ritual

The first thing you can do for yourself, from an emotional capacity, is staying committed to your daily mindfulness ritual. Mindfulness is going to help you in countless ways, including processing and releasing emotions. A great way to incorporate mindfulness specifically into your daily emotional management ritual is to use mindfulness to help you recognize what emotions you are experiencing and to navigate them in an intentional capacity. The more mindful you are, the more you will find meaningful ways to address your emotions during your emotional release.

One great way to incorporate mindfulness into your emotional management routine is to take the time to investigate any emotions you have experienced throughout your day mindfully. You can start by noticing one to three emotions you may have experienced that day that was particularly strong for you. Do not work through any more than three at a time, though, as you do not want to overwhelm yourself and make it more challenging for you to address your emotions.

Once you have noticed these emotions, give yourself time to analyze why they occurred, what happened once they did, and how the aftermath of those emotions was experienced. If you can identify the trigger of the emotions, understand your thoughts and feelings in response to those emotions, and recognize how they lead to your behavior. This will give you a greater understanding of how those emotions affected you. Likewise, if you can acknowledge your emotions'emotions' consequences, you can create the opportunity for you to understand how your emotional responses affected you in the long run. Be sure to do this for both negative and positive emotions, as this will give you a chance to identify opportunities for growth while also giving you a chance to celebrate yourself for growth you have already implemented.

Take Up Journaling

Journaling is a wonderful practice for many different reasons. Aside from helping you keep a little log of your life, journaling allows you to express your true thoughts and emotions outside of yourself, where you otherwise may not have been able to. Many people talk about what they truly think and feel seems impossible, even if they are talking to someone such a therapist where it seems like you "should" be able to speak honestly about what you are thinking or feeling. Having a private journal that you keep to yourself can be a great way for you to openly admit to how you were truly feeling, what you were truly thinking, and anything else that you may have hidden during your day. You can also honestly reflect on what you think and feel after the fact.

Releasing your thoughts from your mind and physically getting them out onto paper may not be quite the same as talking to someone about your emotions, but it will provide you with a great opportunity to get a sense of release. In many cases, the sooner you can release your feelings by admitting them, and the more honestly you can do so, the easier it will be for you to let go and move on in the long run. However, if you get into the habit of acknowledging your emotions and then repressing them, it will become more challenging for you to release how you feel about that particular situation. Hence, the pent up experience begins.

If you are not someone who typically journals, rest assured that there does not need to be a right way or a wrong way for you to engage in journaling. You do not have to be thoughtful, emotional, curious, or well-articulated to keep a journal. You also do not need to worry about spelling, grammar, punctuation, or other writing errors. You don't even need to worry about writing full form sentences, sharing things in story form, or otherwise being exhaustive in what you are thinking and feeling. Even just keeping bullet-point styled notes about what you were thinking and feeling and how that impacted you can be plenty to help you sort through what is going on in your brain. Use your journal in a way that works for you, and trust that this will be plenty to help you fully accept, learn from, and release any emotions you have experienced on a day to day basis.

Give Yourself Frequent Stress Breaks

I firmly believe that stress breaks should be a mandatory part of everyone's daily activities. Day to day life can be stressful, even if you are doing the same thing every day. The demands of work-life, family life and other parts of life can all be overwhelming, even on the best of days. Giving yourself stress breaks means that you are willing to acknowledge your emotional state and make choices that will nurture your wellbeing. When it comes to emotional management, there is no one size fits all. Spending just one session working on your emotions each day will not result in you having effortless or healthy emotional expressions for the rest of the day. It will improve your chances. However, you still need to make choices that will keep you in a healthy state of expression during the day. You can improve your expressions on a day to day basis by being willing to give yourself stress breaks so that you can decompress.

A stress break could be an intentionally scheduled break where you get to do something different from your normal activities. However, a stress break can also be accomplished by giving yourself 5-10 minutes to decompress anytime you find yourself feeling particularly stressed or emotionally charged during the day. You can also give yourself 5-10 minutes to decompress if you find yourself feeling drained or overdrawn from your day. During those 5-10 minutes, allow yourself time to simply breathe, be mindful, and engage in a relaxing routine that will allow you to feel more at peace after your day. Through this, you will find yourself flowing much more peacefully and harmoniously throughout your day.

Work In Harmony With Your Nature

Whenever you try to do something, it is always best to work with your nature rather than against it. In particular, with emotions, working with your nature means rather than denying your emotions or trying to force them to change, you learn to incorporate them into your daily experience. Incorporating your emotions into your daily routines could include fitting certain parts of your routines into certain parts of your day and scheduling your days based on how your feelings behave.

When it comes to scheduling with your energy, consider how you tend to have energy during the day and schedule your activities based on that. This way, you are not trying to force yourself to engage in things when you do not have adequate energy for them. Therefore you have no reason to feel pressured or stressed in those activities. For example, if you know that you tend to have more energy in the morning and less in the evening, you could exercise in the morning and do your mindfulness routine in the evening. If, however, you are the opposite and you tend to have less energy in the morning and more in the evening, you might benefit from doing your mindfulness practice in the morning and exercising in the evening. This way, you are working with your nature to create harmony and flow throughout your day, and you are not amplifying your stress for any reason.

You can also schedule your days based on how you anticipate you will feel. For example, let's say you are trying to schedule your week out, and you know that you have a stressful project to complete on Tuesday. Based on this knowledge, you might make Monday and Tuesday relatively relaxing days and save other things, such as cleaning the house or engaging in other demanding activities later, once the project has already been finished. This way, rather than forcing yourself to get anything done when you already know that you won't have the energy, you work with your nature instead.

As far as emotional fulfillment efforts go, focus on learning tools that allow you to release emotions in a way that can easily be executed on a day to day basis. Exercise, art, listening to music, relaxing, talking to a loved one, and other similar measures can all be used to release your emotions in a healthy, productive manner. Suppose you tend to experience many rapid emotions during the day. In that case, you might even consider carrying a journal with you and quickly jotting things down anytime you come across a large feeling. This way, you can quickly release that feeling at the moment, and you can reasonably circle back to it later on in the day. This would be far healthier than, say, stuffing it down and allowing it to ruin the rest of your day.

Conclusion

Mastering and regulating your emotions are a question of choice. You either want to do it or you don't. There's no shortage of information about the subject of emotions, yet many still struggle with control over this aspect.

Learning to master your emotions is like learning a new skill or habit. Having to change the way that you've been accustomed to doing something is not easy.

You know you don't want to be at the mercy of your emotions forever.

So, it's time to work on what you can do about it. When emotions hit you like a tidal wave at the beach, the first habit you need to put a stop to is instinctively trying to dismiss them.

Stop sweeping your feelings under the rug or trying to run away from them. Your emotions need your attention. Instead of fleeing your emotions, you need to face them with self-control and emotional resilience.

In an overly stressful situation, your ability to effectively regulate your impulsive behavior, control it, and not succumb to the temptation reacting in a way you know to be negative, that is emotional self-control. Without emotional self-control, it will be easy to end up in a lot of trouble because of your poor reactions. In a professional setting, a lack of emotional self-control will be extremely damaging to your career prospects. Would you elect someone emotionally volatile into a leadership role? Or task them with more responsibility? The answer is no, not when you know they could have an emotional meltdown at any moment.

Being mindful and aware of your emotions will serve you well in the development of your emotional self-control capabilities. That's the reason self-awareness is the first core EI skill that needs to be developed. It enables you to cultivate the necessary awareness needed about the sequence of events leading to the emotion you feel.

The key to emotional self-control is to learn how to manage your emotions. Manage, being the focus word here to clarify that this is not about suppressing your emotions. Exercising self-control over your emotions is giving yourself the time and space needed to work through your challenging emotions so you can stay calm even in the face of emotions that threaten to destabilize you.

Learning control in this aspect matters more than you think. As the brain's radar in charge of detecting potential threats, the amygdala has the power to "hijack" your brain and take over when it goes into overdrive. In this hijacked state, the only thing that your brain can focus on is what is causing you distress. You can't focus on your job, you can't focus on a conversation, you can't focus on anything except the perceived threat that the amygdala has zoned in. When you can't focus and think clearly, that's when mistakes happen.

As you learn to develop your emotional self-control, each successful attempt will boost your confidence, reinforcing the belief that you can do this. A boost in confidence leads to the development of self-esteem. There's a feeling of pride and a sense of accomplishment that follows when you know you've overcome what you thought you couldn't do. To successfully wrestle control back from your emotions and put yourself in the driver's seat again was not easy, but you did it anyway and you should be proud.

Emotional intelligence is not a subject you're going to find taught in schools, although it should be, given what a beneficial skill it can be. In a world where anxiety and stress are at in its prime, EI skills are by far the most important skill anyone can learn because of its strong connection to your sense of self. When everything in life doesn't feel like an emotional roller coaster that's threatening to spin out of control, it transcends into your life's other aspects. Your relationships are better, you feel better, and you're infused with a strong, healthy sense of self-esteem because of that newfound control.

Emotional management is also an incredibly powerful tool to help you begin to experience true happiness and fulfillment in your life. So often, people get stuck in negative cycles where their emotions feel overwhelming and seem to take over, and that can lead to massive levels of guilt, embarrassment, and shame. The more you feel those emotions, and reinforce them through your emotional expressions, the more you will find yourself struggling to feel true happiness and fulfillment in your life. When you learn to change those behaviors, however, you begin to create space for you to heal from past emotional expressions and enjoy healthier and more fulfilling new ones. Through that, you begin to experience emotional freedom, as well as true happiness and fulfillment in your life.

Low self-esteem invokes negative feelings and emotions. When all you can think about are the worst things about yourself and all the things and life, you fail to regulate your emotions properly, and dwelling in unhappiness for too long is how your self-esteem starts to diminish. Your emotions are not the only powerful thing at your disposal. Your mental toughness is also a very powerful asset that you possess. By constantly pursuing betterment in your life overall, you'll find more things to be happy about, which leads to higher levels of satisfaction. The way you feel about yourself starts to improve and with it, your self-esteem.

Developing Greater Self-Esteem, Self-Awareness and Emotional Resilience

Life is always going to be full of ups and downs. Even if you're happy in general, there may be some moments where you encounter difficult or trying times. In the face of these challenging situations, there are only two options to choose from:

·   Option 1 - You can either run away and let your emotions strip you of happiness.

·   Option 2 - You can choose to be emotionally resilient and bounce back from these trying times. To see the challenges as an opportunity for self-improvement.

Emotional resilience is what emotionally intelligent people turn to when hard times befall them. Instead of letting their emotions consume them, they choose to learn from them. Emotionally resilient people don't let their unhappy emotions define who they are, and they use emotional self-control and self-esteem to do it. When times are the hardest, resilience keeps you going.

Self-esteem is an important component of resilience. When you lack it, it makes a big difference in your perspective of life. When self-esteem is present, it's easier to feel optimistic, cheerful and overall more positive outlook towards the different areas of your life. Positivity is the key to successful resilience. When times are hard, that's when you need positivity and optimism to fall back on or it would feel all too easy to succumb to the temptation of giving up. Without self-esteem and a strong belief in yourself, it will feel impossible to weather the emotional storms that come your way. Believing that you can make it through the battle is halfway towards winning it. Like your emotions, self-esteem is going to fluctuate. Some days you might feel more confident than others.

Building a strong foundation of self-esteem and self-control is how you master emotional resilience, and here's what you need to do to start mastering these skills:

- Find A Healthy Outlet - Find a healthy outlet that works for you to channel your emotions. This outlet should be something that makes you feel good about yourself again and feel better after an emotional time. It could be yoga, meditating, listening to music, exercising, catching up with a loved one, etc.
- Build A Support System - Talking to someone you can trust who won't judge you in return can be the antidote to an emotional, troubled soul. Not everyone may be lucky enough to form these close relationships, so it is okay to seek professional help if you feel you might benefit from having someone to talk to.
- Persevere - Resilience is about not giving up no matter how much you may be tempted to. Build on your resilience, self-esteem, and self-control by pushing yourself to keep taking one step forward, no matter how hard it feels at first. Trust that you're getting better with each step forward and you'll emerge victorious, confident and resilient at the end.
- Give Yourself Time - Even the most painful wounds can heal when given enough time. Without self-esteem, resilience, and self-control, emotions get out of control when you're hurt and pain. Be patient, take each day as

it comes and remember that you will get through this and feel better. All you need to do is give yourself time.

- Happiness Is Your Choice - It is a choice that only you can make for yourself each day. Emotionally resilient people choose to prioritize their happiness over every other emotion, and they're a lot more confident and in control because of that choice.

Thank you for taking time reading this book and I hope you learn so much on how to master your emotions!

CPSIA information can be obtained
at www.ICGtesting.com
Printed in the USA
BVHW041541160221
600148BV00020B/250